Heaven & Hell

An in-depth view

Pastor Bruce A. Shields

HEAVEN & HELL

An in-depth view

House of Faith Publishing
219 Adams St.
East Tawas, MI. 48730

www.PS127.org

Requests for information should be addressed to:
House of Faith Publishing
219 Adams St.
East Tawas, MI. 48730
www.PS127.org

All Scripture quotations, unless otherwise indicated, are taken from the *King James Holy Bible.*

Shields, Pastor Bruce A.
Heaven & Hell – An in-depth view / Pastor Bruce A. Shields.

Second Edition – March 2019
Third Edition – October 2022

Printed in the United States of America

House of Faith Publishing
www.ps127.org - *www.BruceShields.us*

[Acknowledgments]

MY UTMOST APPRECIATION TO…

The Lord Jesus Christ, who through the Holy Spirit has called me out of the world and into the Kingdom, has incredibly blessed my life and given me through revelation a calling to be a pillar in His church, the Body of Christ, to serve as one who preaches and teaches His Word to His People.

To Terri, my wife, without whom I could not adequately serve Christ. She has been with me and by my side through all things and continues to be a blessing to our children and me.

I also dedicate this book to my Church family at the House of Faith. Dedicated to serving the Lord Jesus Christ and standing on His Word, being the salt of the earth, by staying pure to His Word. Being a light to the community by offering their love for others as the Word instructs, and for their commitment to Christ by sharing the Gospel with the world to be a lighthouse, bringing others into the Body of Christ and fulfilling God's Will.

To the countless others who, through their love and friendships, have strengthened me and lifted me as brothers and sisters in Christ through the gifts they have received and used to build and edify the Body of Christ.

I hope that through examining where we as a people were, we can discover through the scriptures where we are going and, through that find the only truth that matters in this world, and that is salvation through faith in the one, true and eternal Lord, Jesus Christ.

[Contents]

[Chapters]

[FOREWORD]

One may ask the question, "Why did God create angels and us with the ability to sin against Him?" The answer to this question may be easier than it sounds. God created us with what is commonly called 'free will.' What is the purpose of this? The objective is to worship Him and love Him because we want to, not because we are His robots. If God wanted, He could have made billions of pre-programmed little robots that never stumble and worship continually without ceasing. But there cannot be love if there is no free will.

You cannot truly love if you do not have the ability to "not love." The same goes for worship and righteousness. You cannot truly worship if you do not have the ability to "not worship." And you cannot be righteous if you do not have the ability to be "unrighteous."

For this reason, after creating all in the garden and it was good, the ability for the fall was also placed in the garden. At that moment, Adam and Eve were righteous until they ate the forbidden tree's fruit. If the tree had never been created, there would be no ability for Adam or Eve to sin. Therefore they couldn't be righteous because it was impossible to be unrighteous. When there is no choice, there is no free will.

I think we have all had the occasion at one time or another to experience a robotic association, where you and the other person go through the motions in a relationship but never truly connect. Then down the road, when we are blessed in a godly relationship, we discover what true love and relationship are. There is a noticeable difference between actively loving and going through the robotic motions.

God wants this "godly" relationship with us as "free will love" because we want to love Him, not because we were programmed to.

OK, so you ask, with this being so, "Why do those who are unrighteous and sinful have to go to eternal damnation? Why can't they just NOT exist anymore if they can't go to heaven?"

God created us in the beginning with souls that are everlasting so that we could exist with Him for eternity to come. Although our souls have a beginning, they do not have an end. This is why the term everlasting is used as opposed to eternal. God is eternal; He has no beginning or end. But we were created. Therefore our souls are everlasting. We all have this, whether righteous or unrighteous, because we were designed to be with God. It is God's will that ALL come to a knowledge of the Truth and are saved.

Simply put, we were created to be with God for eternity. And we know from the scriptures that God does not change His word. If He were to act in contradiction to His Word, He would be a liar.

If He were to end the existence of anything that He had created as everlasting, then He would be, in essence, calling Himself a liar. So what He calls everlasting MUST be everlasting, regardless of their behavior or where they end up for eternity. And it is for this purpose that an everlasting holding place for the unrighteous and sinful was created.

The question in our life is not whether or not we are going to be resurrected and given an everlasting body because that has already been designated for each of us. When we die, we WILL be resurrected and given an everlasting body.

The real question is, after you receive your everlasting body, where are you going to spend the rest of eternity with it?

We know that it is God's will that all humankind come to Him to be with the Lord for eternity. But because of 'free will,' not everyone will submit themselves to the Lord.

This is a sad but true point of existence. From this point in time onward, we will exist forever in eternity with everlasting bodies. The only question you have to ask is, "Where am I going to be?"

I heard someone once say, Salvation is FREE. To follow Christ costs us little. But to serve Christ costs us everything!

If you have never given yourself to our Lord and Creator, it is simple to do. Christ wants a personal one-on-one relationship with YOU! All you need to do is accept Jesus as the Son of God, who came and died for you and three days later rose again. Confess that you are sinful. We all are! And commit yourself to the Lord, and He will change your life for eternity!

If you want to learn more about salvation or our Lord, please feel free to visit ***www.TruthDigest.org*** or ***www.PS127.org***

Our Lord and Savior is coming back! Be watchful! Be prepared!

Praise the Lord!

[INTRODUCTION]

This book is the result of years of study on the subject of heaven and hell. It began as a simple question asked by a student in a class I was teaching years ago. We were studying a course I took in Seminary entitled 'The House of Faith,' which incidentally, a few years later, became the name of the ministry I started with my wife in late 2002.

I was explicitly teaching the subject of salvation and Christ as the foundation and how it was directly related to our life on earth and destination afterward when one of the students asked the simple question, "Where do we go when we die?"

Of course, I answered with, "**6** *Therefore we are always confident, knowing that, whilst we are at home in the body, we are absent from the Lord:* **7** *(For we walk by faith, not by sight :)* **8** *We are confident, I say, and willing rather to be absent from the body, and to be present with the Lord."* - **2 *Corinthians 5:6 – 8***

She replied, "Doesn't the Bible say that Christ is the *ONLY* way to heaven?"

Again, I felt this question to be an easy one and answered, "Yes." ***John 14:6***

Looking confused, she asked one more question. "Then where did everyone go who died before Christ?"

This is where everything came to a screeching halt. Now the rest of the class was just as perplexed as she.

Nearly four years of Seminary and many years of independent studies, which included personal as well as interdenominational, and to my recollection, none honestly addressed this question head-on and gave a straight answer. But, as teachers, we are placed in a position to know everything, or at least expected to, which can sometimes be frustrating.

We also know that as teachers of the Word, we are held to higher accountability to the Word of God, and one must be SURE before one speaks on things such as these.

After a moment of thought, I concluded that I would research the question and give her an answer in the following class.

As I began to research, I realized that this was a subject that most shy away from. Still, I wanted to give a straight answer, as opposed to many who teach the Word, who tend to provide loop-hole solutions that seemingly answer everything generically.

One such response would be, "You don't HAVE to know. It's about FAITH!" as if you lack faith because you have a question.

So many times, I see teachers avoid answers and place the burden on those who are seeking instead of admitting there is something they may not understand themselves.

Jesus said, "Seek me and you WILL FIND." We must let believers know that it is not a 'lack of faith' to want real answers to real questions. That in itself is SEEKING, just as Jesus tells us to do.

It is no fault of the student because a teacher is ill-prepared to answer as we are commanded to be ready to do in the Word.

So many times, people want to burden the seeker because they lack understanding or integrity, especially when it comes to answered prayers, healings, and such.

If something doesn't work out, it always seems to be, "Well, sir or madam; you just didn't have enough faith.", or to paraphrase, "The power of God isn't working in your life because you aren't DOING something right."

So I took all the available resources and searched the scriptures, comparing every scripture to the original Hebrew and Greek text.

By the next class, I had to disappoint everyone with the news that I needed a little more time to research the matter further because of the amount of material I had to go through.

I wanted to ensure an accurate and proper answer that came from the scriptures alone and left out personal opinions.

Nearly two years later, I had not only compiled pages and pages of research and scriptures but also put them together in a way that I believe is easy to understand. I have also included original charts that I have created from information given in the scriptures to help illustrate what the Word is telling us about the afterlife and the order of what is to come.

I split this information into two major sections: where the Old Testament man went when he died and why, and where the New Testament man goes when he dies.

I have also shown how the theory of any purgatory is scripturally false doctrine and explained why this notion of a road to heaven leading through hell is not only contrary to scripture but degrading to Christ's atoning sacrifice.

Please contact me with any comments or questions by mail or email. My address is in the back of the book. Also, suppose you have any additional scriptures that fit in any part of this book. In that case, I am always looking for more information to make this a complete study and would love to hear from you.

Also, please remember that no one *person* completely understands the entire word of God, and I am in no way trying to portray myself as someone who does.

This is an area where not many Theologians have wanted to step in fear of criticism from colleges and skeptics here and abroad.

I have the luxury of not caring what anyone but God thinks of me and my attempt at understanding His Holy Word. I have studied and re-studied these scriptures in hopes of coming to a sound doctrine taught to us by our Lord. Praise the Lord!

[CHAPTER ONE]

INTRODUCTION - Old Testament Man

To get a correct understanding of heaven and hell, it is necessary to distinguish between the *past, present, and future abodes of the dead.* We must also get proper knowledge of the words as they are used in the *original Hebrew and Greek texts* and not as the translators have rendered them in the King James Version (as well as many other translations) to make them easier to read or through improper translation.

It would be impossible to arrive at an accurate understanding of death, heaven, and hell, from any English Translations, except for some literal translations, without first going directly to the original Hebrew and Greek.

A friend of mine once made the statement to me, "Isn't it awesome how Jesus went to *Hell* for three days and then came back?" Did Jesus go to Hell? My friend was probably reading a King James Version of the Bible in the book of Acts, where there is a reference to Christ in hell.

"He seeing this before spake of the resurrection of Christ, that his soul was not left in hell, neither his flesh did see corruption." ***Acts 2:31***

But the word used in the original text was Hades, which is the Greek equivalent of Sheol, which means 'place of departed souls.'

Sheol is the place for *ALL* the departed souls (in Old Testament times), righteous and unrighteous, separated by a vast gulf.

Torment was for the unrighteous dead, and Abraham's bosom (or Paradise) was for the righteous dead. Abraham's bosom is where Christ went to minister to those who had died and were "gathered unto their fathers."

So Jesus didn't go to *Hell*. Instead, he went to Sheol into Abraham's bosom. But we will speak about all of this later. First, we need to discuss why there are discrepancies in the King James Bible when it is compared to the original texts.

The King James Version of the Bible resulted from the Hampton Court Conference in 1604 when King James I of England agreed to a suggestion that a new translation of the Holy Scriptures should be created. King James was at this time trying to mend relations between the religious parties in his kingdom, so he agreed to the project of one Bible for public worship services of the Church of England. Forty-seven (Anglican) of that day's finest Hebrew and Greek scholars were divided into three groups. They worked over two years, and in 1611 the Bible known as the Authorized Version was published, even though the King never officially authorized the final version. This was the best English Bible produced to that date, and for 300 years, this was the Bible used by the entire English-speaking world.

Although most of the language is now outdated because it was written in 17th-century English. It has been calculated that approximately 300 words used in the King James Version had a different meaning than today.

The King James Version of the Holy Bible is based on the *'Textus Receptus'* manuscripts. However, much older and more significant manuscripts have been discovered since its translation. Manuscript discoveries since the sixteenth century have given us knowledge of the original texts because they were created closer to the originals. Still, there have been many debates over their use of them.

Some argue they are more accurate and reliable, while others claim the text is complete 'as is.' I believe, though, most of the textual variants have no real effect on the doctrine, which in essence, makes the debate pointless.

Either way, we do not have *Actual* documents written by the original authors. We only have many copies of the manuscripts that must be compared to each other to discover any discrepancies. I feel that there is a reason God did not want the original manuscripts to survive the centuries. Still, His Word and Will *HAS* survived in the thousands of ancient copies of them.

I believe that the original manuscripts did not survive because, like so many other *objects* throughout history, people tend to worship the item as opposed to the God who created it. I feel that the power of the scriptures may have been attributed to the scriptures themselves instead of God's Word contained within them. We see this mentality around the world with worshiping items such as statues, shrouds, and just about anything that can be linked to a religious person or event.

It breaks my heart when I see people lining up to touch statues of the saints in hopes of miraculous healing. This is idol worship. There is no power in stone. Regardless of whom the stone supposedly looks like.

One thing we must keep in mind about the differences between the King James Version and the original texts, the authors in no way intended to mislead the readers. It is merely a matter of the evolution of communication and speech.

When we compare the King James Version with the Original texts (original simply meaning the oldest manuscripts we have today), the following differences;

	KJV 1611	**Original Text**
1 Thessalonians 4:15	*Prevent*	*Precede*
Philippians 1:27	*Conversation*	*Conduct*
Romans 1:13	*Let*	*Hindered*
2 Corinthians 6:12	*Bowels*	*Feelings*

We see from this comparison that the meanings of a few words have changed over the past few hundred years, significantly altering the meaning of these scriptures. From these examples, one can see that it is *us* and our language that has changed over the centuries altering translations, not the Word of God.

The original Hebrew, Aramaic & Greek text was, without error or contradiction, breathed by the Spirit of God, not the translations that have been written and rewritten throughout the years.

And these are but a few of the many examples of differences in our language.
It's even more evident in all the "thee's" and "thou's" throughout the scriptures in the King James Version.

Neither this book nor I am trying to discredit or attack the King James Version of the Holy Bible or any of the other many English translations because of their translational or paraphrased errors. On the contrary, I use various translations regularly for reading and studying. But we must remember that because *OUR* language, speech, and definitions of words change with our culture over time, we must be willing to compare these translations with the Original Hebrew and Greek texts for an accurate reading and understanding of the scripture if we are to indulge in any serious study of the Holy Word.

I will give a few examples of this King James translation dilemma, but this only reflects a small percentage of the actual translation differences from the original Hebrew and Greek texts.

Why even show these examples? To illustrate "why," there is much confusion about heaven and hell. Most of the confusion can be traced back to poor translations.

I merely want to illustrate that specific changes have been made from the original text because of language barriers when translating from one language to another and differences in the meanings of words that have changed significantly over the centuries.

EXAMPLE 1

***Matthew* 23:33**
"Ye serpents, ye generation of vipers, how can ye escape the damnation of hell?"

Here we see the word *hell* is used in this scripture to replace the original text Hebrew word *Gehenna*. Here, Jesus condemns the religious leaders of the day for their behavior and warns them of their future. He references the Hebrew word *Gehenna* in the original Greek text to illustrate what the final *hell*, or second death, would be like. *Gehenna* was a valley of Hinnom in Jerusalem which was widely known, which is why it was used allegorically by Jesus as the name for the place of everlasting punishment. But we'll get more into that in later chapters. The point here is the original text Hebrew word *Gehenna* is replaced by the King James translators simply as *hell.*

EXAMPLE 2

Luke 16:22-23

"And it came to pass, that the beggar died, and was carried by the angels into Abraham's bosom: the rich man also died, and was buried; And in hell he lift up his eyes, being in torments, and seeth Abraham afar off, and Lazarus in his bosom."

Again, we see Jesus talking here about the rich man and the beggar, who both have died. But according to the King James Version, the rich man can see Abraham and the beggar Lazarus in hell.

Well, we know from reading the scripture that angels carried Lazarus to Abraham's bosom, and the rich man just died and opened his eyes in torment.

Would righteous Abraham be in *hell* with the unfaithful rich man? Of course not, yet they can see each other. *Hell* replaces the original Greek word *Hades,* which literally means *'the place for departed souls.'*

So the faithful and righteous as well as the unfaithful and unrighteous, went to the same place when they died in the Old Testament, and that was to *Hades,* or as the Old Testament called it, *Sheol,* which means *'the place of departed souls.'*

We see that though the righteous and unrighteous both went to *Sheol,* the place of departed souls, or those who have died, the side of torments for the wicked that the rich man was in is separate from the side of Abraham's bosom reserved for the righteous.

Luke 16:23
"And in hell he lifted up his eyes, being in torments, and seeth Abraham afar off, and Lazarus in his bosom

Luke 16:26
"And beside all this, between us and you there is a great gulf fixed: so that they which would pass from here to you cannot; neither can they pass to us that would come from there."

So even though the rich man, Abraham, and Lazarus were all in *Sheol,* there were two different locations. Abraham's bosom for the righteous and torment for the unrighteous.

So translating *Sheol* into the word *hell* is improper here by our English understanding, considering to most people, the word hell means the place of punishment for the unrighteous. This is why it is difficult for many to understand what Sheol is.

EXAMPLE 3

2 Peter 2:4
"For if God spared not the angels that sinned, but cast them down to hell, and delivered them into chains of darkness, to be reserved unto judgment;"

Here the word *hell* is again generically used by the King James translators to describe the place where the angels that sinned were cast. The word that was used here in the original text, though, is *Tartarus,* which means *'the deepest Abyss below Sheol,'* and *'to incarcerate in eternal torment.'*

So this place, Tartarus, is entirely different from the place of torment because it is defined as *'the deepest Abyss below Sheol,'* and we read earlier in scripture that you can see Abraham's bosom from torment, which is never mentioned about Tartarus. Yet the King James translators again used the word hell.

CONCLUSION

You can see from the examples given that *Sheol (Hades), Gehenna, Torment, Abraham's Bosom, Paradise,* and *Tartarus* are the names of distinctly different places which serve different purposes, but were all translated into the single word *hell* in the King James Version of the Holy Bible.

This is one of the reasons for our current confusion about what hell is, where it is, and precisely what God created it for.

This book will attempt to clarify the roles of each place that God has set aside for His specific purpose, and examine with scripture using the original Hebrew and Greek text for clarity what that purpose was and what roles the locations play today, if any.

The following chapters will explain each location, showing multiple scriptures so that we can conclude that the roles and locations are scriptural and not conjecture. But, of course, we must keep in mind that with all Biblical study, we must rely on the Holy Spirit for understanding and remember that we will never completely understand the mind of God. That is until we see Him face to face.

He is perfect, Holy, and beyond our human experience and comprehension. His word to us is His Holy hand reaching into a fallen world to lift those up who call on His most precious Son's name to be saved. This study and this book are intended for a deeper understanding of God and His plan, not an explanation of how the universe operates or how God works.

[CHAPTER TWO]

LIFE - Living for God's Purpose

[Faithful and Righteous]

In this chapter, we will discuss what God considers to be faithful and righteous. This is the Old Testament equivalent of being a born-again Christian. We will cover some scriptures where God shows us the behavior He expects for righteousness. Because God is a righteous and fair judge, we will also explore what God says is unfaithful and unrighteous behavior. He gives us these examples in His Holy Word, leaving us without an excuse when judgment comes.

Because Israel was selected by God to be the chosen people, He viewed them as His firstborn (***Exodus* 4:22, 23**), which not only signified Israel's favored status among the nations to be in a covenant relationship with God but also gave them the responsibilities that were required of the firstborn.

The firstborn is regarded as special (***Genesis 49:3; Exodus 13:2***), and he became the head of the family if the father was absent, having received his father's blessing (***Genesis 27***) and a double portion of the inheritance (***Deuteronomy 21:17***) upon his death.

After the Passover event in Egypt, every firstborn male belonged to God. This implied priestly duties, an obligation later transferred to the Levites (***Numbers 8:14-19***).

Therefore, Israel was responsible for performing the priestly functions as God's saving light to the Gentile people.

In the Old Testament, Israel was expected to respond in faithfulness to God because He had acted faithfully to them throughout the covenant.

David and other godly people in the scriptures chose to walk the faithful way - the way of truth. Just as God is faithful and loving, those who believe in God need to exhibit faithfulness and steadfast love in their lives.

Righteousness in the Old Testament locates its meaning in the sphere of God's gracious, covenantal relation to His people and the appropriate behavior of the covenant partners (Yahweh and Israel) toward each other.

For a more precise understanding, faithfulness and righteousness are following God's leading and Word. We are without excuse. God doesn't expect us to just *know* right and wrong behavior. He tells us what is right and wrong in His Holy Word and expects us to listen.

When He created Adam in the Garden, He told Adam what righteous behavior (i.e., you can eat from any of the trees in the garden) was. He told Adam what was unrighteous behavior. (i.e., you may NOT eat of the tree of knowledge).

When we do not obey, this places us in an area of disobedience (unrighteousness) where God's protection, benefits, and blessings do not exist.

When we disobey, we step off the proverbial 'narrow path' (***Matthew 7:14***), where everything God has planned for us in our lives resides. When we step onto this 'broad road which leads to destruction' (***Matthew 7:13***), we are vulnerable to the 'wiles of the devil' (***Ephesians 6:11***) and need to return, or repent, so that we may be in God's protection, which takes place in our obedience in being 'doers of the Word.'

One of the best scriptures to illustrate how God holds us responsible and accountable for our behavior is, again, one of the first illustrations in the Bible, Adam and the Word of god.

Genesis 3:9-19

"And the Lord God called unto Adam, and said unto him, Where art thou? And he said, I heard thy voice in the garden, and I was afraid, because I was naked; and I hid myself. And he said, who told thee that thou wast naked? Hast thou eaten of the tree, whereof I commanded thee that thou shouldest not eat? And the man said, the woman whom thou gavest to be with me, she gave me of the tree, and I did eat. And the Lord God said unto the woman, what is this that thou hast done? And the woman said, the serpent beguiled me, and I did eat. And the Lord God said unto the serpent, Because thou hast done this, thou art cursed above all cattle, and above every beast of the field; upon thy belly shalt thou go, and dust shalt thou eat all the days of thy life: And I will put enmity between thee and the woman, and between thy seed and her seed; it shall bruise thy head, and thou shalt bruise his heel. Unto the woman he said, I will greatly multiply thy sorrow and thy conception; in sorrow thou shalt bring forth children; and thy desire shall be to thy husband, and he shall rule over thee. And unto Adam he said, Because thou hast hearkened unto the voice of thy wife, and hast eaten of the tree,

of which I commanded thee, saying, Thou shalt not eat of it: cursed is the ground for thy sake; in sorrow shalt thou eat of it all the days of thy life; Thorns also and thistles shall it bring forth to thee; and thou shalt eat the herb of the field; In the sweat of thy face shalt thou eat bread, till thou return unto the ground; for out of it wast thou taken: for dust thou art, and unto dust shalt thou return."

Adam blamed Eve, then God for giving him Eve. Eve blamed the devil. All three sinned, yet no one wanted to accept the blame. But God held each accountable, not just for the sin of eating from the tree. Still, He punished each of them individually for their participation in sin.

We have a responsibility as well as accountability for our behavior. God is a just God who handed out judgment to the individual for their part in the sinful act.

Though we may try to ultimately blame someone else or some circumstance for our actions or decisions and even our behavior, we are the ones who God will deal with individually as He did in the garden that day.

Following the order of what happened, God also handed out punishments. First to the devil for his part, then to the woman for hers, and lastly to the foolish man who could have put a stop to the fall of humankind right there but chose to listen to his flesh instead of God's Will.

Another critical point to keep in mind while we study righteous and faithful behavior is that God doesn't change. Neither does His character. Nor does what He expects from us. We see in Deuteronomy a list of characteristics God expected His people to have in the Old Testament.

We also see in the following scripture that we are to obey the commandments of the Lord. This fact was repeated by our Lord in the New Testament,

"If you love me, you will obey my commands." ***John 14:15***

Deuteronomy 10:12-13
"And now, Israel, what doth the Lord thy God require of thee, but to fear the Lord thy God, to walk in all His ways, and to love Him, and to serve the Lord thy God with all thy heart and with all thy soul, to keep the commandments of the Lord, and His statutes, which I command thee this day for thy good?"

Here God states to us what He considers righteous and faithful behavior. We must fear, or hold in reverence, the Lord. We must walk in all His ways. We must love and serve God with all of our heart and soul. And we must keep the Lord's commandments and statutes.

This applies even today. I often hear people say, "But that was in the Old Testament!" as if God has somehow changed in light of His creation? On the contrary, we know from scripture that God is immutable, unchangeable in nature or purpose.

Psalms 33:11
"The counsel of the Lord standeth forever, the thoughts of His heart to all generations."

Proverbs 19:21
"There are many devices in a man's heart; nevertheless the counsel of the Lord, that shall stand."

Ecclesiastes 3:14
"I know that, whatsoever God doeth, it shall be for ever: nothing can be put to it, nor any thing taken from it: and God doeth it, that men should fear before Him."

Isaiah 14:24
"The Lord of hosts hath sworn, saying, Surely as I have thought, so shall it come to pass; and as I have purposed, so shall it stand:"

Ezekiel 24:14
"I the Lord have spoken it: it shall come to pass, and I will do it; I will not go back, neither will I spare, neither will I repent; according to thy ways, and according to thy doings, shall they judge thee, saith the Lord God."

Romans 11:29
"For the gifts and calling of God are without repentance."

James 1:17
"Every good gift and every perfect gift is from above, and cometh down from the Father of lights, with whom is no variableness, neither shadow of turning."

This is why Salvation through the atoning sacrifice of Jesus Christ is so important because there are only two covenants with man.

Law, by which all men are guilty, the covenant of Christ, and His atoning sacrifice, which pays the debt we owe, allowing us to be found innocent on judgment day instead of guilty.

If you do not have a covenant with Jesus Christ, you will be held accountable to the covenant of Law, by which you will be found guilty.

So it's very evident from scripture that there is no repentance (turning from or changing direction) in the thoughts or actions of God. With this in mind, we know that what God expected from the Old Testament man, as far as behavior toward Himself and others, is still expected today. It was Jesus who said the following;

***Matthew* 5:17**
"Think not that I am come to destroy the law, or the prophets: I am come not to destroy, but to fulfill."

Jesus made it clear. God's moral and ceremonial laws were given to help people love God with all of their hearts and minds. But these laws, over time, had been misquoted and misapplied. As a result, by Jesus' time, the religious leaders had turned the laws into a confusing mess of rules and regulations.

When Jesus taught, though it was new to everyone then, He was trying to steer everyone back to God's *original* plan. Jesus never spoke against the law itself but often against the abuses of and excesses to which the religious leaders of the day had taken it.

In Jesus' Sermon on the Mount, He tightened the Law where humankind had loosened it. He gave the correct interpretation of the Word of God, which was easy for Him to do, considering He is the Word made flesh.

The Law or Commandments were not given to justify man but to show his need for a savior because God's standards are above ours.

Here are some scriptures that help us understand what God expects from His people.

Psalms 1:1-3
"Blessed is the man that walketh not in the counsel of the ungodly, nor standeth in the way of sinners, nor sitteth in the seat of the scornful. But his delight is in the law of the Lord; and in His law doth he meditate day and night. And he shall be like a tree planted by the rivers of water, that bringeth forth fruit in his season; his leaf also shall not wither; and whatsoever he doeth shall prosper."

This theme is continued throughout the scriptures, giving many examples of righteous and faithful behavior. We are warned against spending time with the ungodly and against keeping people from making their own choices and exercising their '*free will*' given to us by God. We must also act in love in our actions as opposed to one who is hateful. We must meditate on God's word day and night, measuring our thoughts and deeds by it.

Psalms 15

"Lord, who shall abide in thy tabernacle? Who shall dwell in the holy hill? He that walketh uprightly, and worketh righteousness, and speaketh the truth in his heart. He that backbiteth not with his tongue, nor do evil to his neighbor, nor taketh up a reproach against his neighbor. In whose eyes a vile person is condemned; but he that honoureth them that fear the Lord. He that sweareth to his own hurt, and changeth not. He that putteth not out his money to usery, nor taketh reward against the innocent. He that doeth these things shall never be moved."

Psalms 119:1-5

"Blessed are the undefiled in the way, who walk in the law of the Lord. Blessed are they that keep His testimonies and that seek Him with the whole heart. They also do no iniquity: they walk in His ways. Thou hast commanded us to keep they precepts diligently. O that my ways were directed to keep thy statutes!"

Psalms 119:162-176

"I rejoice at thy word, as one that findeth great spoil. I hate and abhor lying: but thy law I do love. Seven times a day do I praise thee because of thy righteous judgments. Great peace have they which love thy law:

and nothing shall offend them. Lord, I have hoped for thy salvation, and done thy commandments. My soul hath kept thy testimonies; and I love them exceedingly. I have kept thy precepts and thy testimonies: for all my ways are before thee. Let my cry come near before thee, O Lord: give me understanding according to thy word. Let my supplication come before thee: deliver me according to thy word. My lips shall utter praise, when thou hast taught me thy statutes. My tongue shall speak of thy word: for all thy commandments are righteousness. Let thine hand help me; for I have chosen thy precepts. I have longed for thy salvation, O Lord; and thy law is my delight. Let my soul live, and it shall praise thee; and let thy judgments help me. I have gone astray like a lost sheep; seek thy servant; for I do not forget thy commandments."

Isaiah 1:17
"Learn to do well; seek judgment, relieve the oppressed, judge the fatherless, plead for the widow."

Here in Isaiah, we read that we are to *learn* to do well. Understanding God's word gives us insight and knowledge. Reading the word teaches us how to do well. We must also help the poor, take charge or lead the fatherless, and take care of widows.

Isaiah 38:19

"The living, he shall praise thee, as I do this day: the father to the children shall make known thy truth."

Here we see that fathers are to raise their children in the word of God, making known to them His truth.

Ezekiel 18:5-9

"But if a man be just, and do that which is lawful and right, And hath not eaten upon the mountains, neither hath lifted up his eyes to the idols of the house of Israel, neither hath defiled his neighbor's wife, neither hath come near to a menstruous woman, And hath not oppressed any, but hath restored to the debtor his pledge, hath spoiled none by violence, hath given his bread to the hungry, and hath covered the naked with a garment; He that hath not given forth upon usury, neither hath taken any increase, that hath withdrawn his hand from iniquity, hath executed true judgment between man and man, Hath walked in my statutes, and hath kept my judgments, to deal truly; he is just, he shall surely live, saith the Lord God."

Micah 6:8

"He hath shewed thee, O man, what is good; and what doth the Lord require of thee, but to do justly, and to love mercy, and to walk humbly with God?"

God has shown us what is right and expected of us in His word. Moreover, he has repeatedly stated the behavior we are to have as righteous and faithful followers of God. Therefore, we are indeed without excuse.

Luke 23:42-43
"And he said unto Jesus, Lord, remember me when thou comest into thy kingdom. And Jesus said unto him, Verily I say unto thee, Today shalt thou be with me in paradise."

Now, some of you reading right now may be asking why I used a New Testament scripture as an illustration in an Old Testament discussion of righteous and faithful behavior.

I did this for two reasons. First of all, Jesus had not died on the cross yet and therefore had not set into motion the effects of His sacrifice for our sins.

So, even though this scripture is documented in the New Testament, it is happening in Old Testament times, under the Old Covenant.

Secondly, God, as we read earlier, is unchanging. Therefore, he determines righteous and faithful behavior in the Old Testament and righteous and faithful behavior now.

In this scripture, we see a thief on the cross calling on the name of the Lord and being saved. He was exclaiming his faith that Jesus was God's son and Lord. He also confessed his guilt a few scriptures back, admitting that he and the other thief deserved to be crucified, but Jesus was innocent. Therefore, Jesus answered his confession and admittance of sin as well as his faith in *who* Christ is by promising to receive him in paradise.

2 Peter 1:5-11

"And beside this, giving all diligence, add to your faith virtue; and to virtue knowledge; and to knowledge temperance; and to temperance patience; and to patience godliness; and to godliness brotherly kindness; and to brotherly kindness charity. For if these things be in you, and abound, they make you that ye shall neither be barren nor unfruitful in the knowledge of our Lord Jesus Christ. But he that lacketh these things is blind, and cannot see afar off, and hath forgotten that he was purged from his old sins. Wherefore the rather, brethren, give diligence to make your calling and election sure: for if ye do these things, ye shall never fall: For so an entrance shall be ministered unto you abundantly into the everlasting kingdom of our Lord and Saviour Jesus Christ." Amen!

[Unfaithful and Unrighteous]

Once we understand what God expects from us, we know what righteous and faithful behavior is. Once you realize what righteous and faithful behavior is, common sense tells you that the opposite would be contrary and considered unrighteous and unfaithful. But God is a just God (***Deuteronomy 32:4***) and would never wrongfully judge anyone. So He also shows us in scripture what unrighteous and unfaithful behavior consists of. Just as He did with Adam, who was judged only for what he knew to be sinful.

I was counseling a married couple many years ago, and the wife thought perhaps she and her husband were being punished by God for some unknown sin in their life. They were both convinced that there was nothing they could think of that they could have done that would cause God to discipline them.

I asked her, "Would you take your child and punish him, not telling him what he had done wrong, and expect him to learn from that experience? What is displeasing to you?" But, of course, the answer is no.

God wouldn't discipline you without you knowing why you were being disciplined. That correction would serve no purpose. You couldn't learn or grow from that experience.

I told her to pray and continue to read God's Word; *if* she were being disciplined, God would reveal it to her because He is a just and fair God.

God chastens us because we are children of God. As a father, He is guiding us to righteousness. Discipline is love.

The Bible tells us in ***Hebrews 12:6*** that the Lord chasteneth us because we are His sons.

Deuteronomy 8:5 *"as a man chasteneth his son, so the Lord chasteneth thee."*

Proverbs 13:24 *"He that spareth his rod hateth his son: but he that loveth him chasteneth him betimes."*

So, being a just and fair God, He doesn't stop telling us *how* we should behave. But he also reveals to us in His word how we should *not* behave.

God shows us what unrighteous and unfaithful behavior is, removing any doubt or guesswork, placing the responsibility of doing right, and holding us accountable without excuse for our actions.

Just like we expect our children to follow specific instructions as parents, God expects the same from us. And God will not hold us to His standards without telling us what His standards are, and they are crystal clear in His Word.

That would be cruel and unjust behavior, which is not part of the characteristics of God taught us in His Holy word.

Psalms 1:4-6
"The ungodly are not so: but are like the chaff which the wind driveth away. Therefore the ungodly shall not stand in the judgment, nor sinners in the congregation of the righteous. For the Lord knoweth the way of the righteous: but the way of the ungodly shall perish."

The unfaithful and unrighteous are like worthless chaff. They will be condemned at the time of judgment because they have no place among the godly. They will be unable to stand on judgment day. They will surely perish.

Psalms 115:17
"The dead praise not the Lord, neither any that go down into silence."

'Down into silence' is a reference to Sheol. This warns that worshiping God *must* take place *before* we die. Because once you die, your eternal fate has been sealed.

Old Testament man would either go to torment or paradise, and there is no praising or worshiping that will change where you are once you go.

Isaiah 38:18 (Lit) *"For Sheol cannot thank you, nor death praise you: they that go down into the pit cannot hope for your truth."*

Here we read another warning to those still alive to praise God now. We see that once you are dead, it's over. The reference to Sheol here is speaking of the torment side because of the reference to the pit and the fact that they have no hope for the coming of Christ the savior (*your Truth*) because when Jesus died (*the crucifixion*), He went to Abraham's bosom (paradise) in Sheol for the faithful and righteous.

Ezekiel 18:10-17
"If he beget a son that is a robber, a shedder of blood, and that doeth the like to any one of these things, And that doeth not any of those duties, but even hath eaten upon the mountains, and defiled his neighbor's wife, Hath oppressed the poor and needy, hath spoiled by violence, hath not restored the pledge, and hath lifted up his eyes to the idols, hath committed abomination, Hath given forth upon usury, and hath taken increase: shall he then live? He shall not live: he hath done all these abominations; he shall surely

die; his blood shall be upon him. Now, lo, if he beget a son, that seeth all his father's sins which he hath done, and considereth, and doeth not such like, That hath not eaten upon the mountains, neither hath lifted up his eyes to the idols of the house of Israel, hath not defiled his neighbor's wife, Neither hath oppressed any, hath not withholding the pledge, neither hath spoiled by violence, but hath given his bread to the hungry, and hath covered the naked with a garment, That hath taken off his hand from the poor, that hath not received usury nor increase, hath executed my judgments, hath walked in my statutes; he shall not die for the iniquity of his father, he shall surely live. As for his father, because he cruelly oppressed, spoiled his brother by violence, and did that which is not good among his people, lo, even he shall die in his iniquity. Yet say ye, Why? doth not the son bear the iniquity of the father? When the son hath done that which is lawful and right, and hath kept all my statutes, and hath done them, he shall surely live. The soul that sinneth, it shall die. The son shall not bear the iniquity of the father; neither shall the father bear the iniquity of the son: the righteousness of the righteous shall be upon him, and the wickedness of the wicked shall be upon him."

Here we see that God holds each of us responsible for knowing His word and accountable for acting on it individually, not holding us accountable to the behavior of our fathers. Although the effects of our father's sins may still be handed down to us, it is not in judgment but rather a consequence, and neither our salvation nor our relationship with God is affected by this. Our salvation and relationship with God are *only* based on our acceptance of God and His word.

EXAMPLE:

A married man commits adultery, and the woman bears a child. This child is a result of the sin of adultery. But, the child may still grow to be a faithful and righteous born-again Christian.

We have a separation from a relationship with God because of Adam's sin in the Garden. We see the visible effects of that sin today due to what happened. Yet, God is righteous and loving and still offers a relationship to us through His Son, Christ Jesus.

Therefore, we still feel the effects of our father Adam's sin. Yet, we can again mend our relationship severed by that sin through Christ Jesus.

Matthew 13:40-42

"As therefore the tares are gathered and burned in the fire; so shall it be in the end of this world. The Son of man shall send forth his angels, and they shall

gather out of his kingdom all things that offend, and them which do iniquity; And shall cast them into a furnace of fire: there shall be wailing and gnashing of teeth."

Here we read of a grim foreshadowing of Gehenna (furnace of fire) reserved for the unfaithful and unrighteous who practice lawlessness. Praise God, He has also secured a place for the righteous and faithful!

[CHAPTER THREE]

DEATH – Is there a hereafter?

The Sadducees denied that the soul lived after death and said there would be no resurrection because of this. They came to Jesus in ***Luke 20:27-40*** to ridicule His doctrine and try to discredit Him.

Luke 20:27-40

"Then came to him certain of the Sadducees, which deny that there is any resurrection; and they asked him, Saying, Master, Moses wrote unto us, If any man's brother die, having a wife, and he die without children, that his brother should take his wife, and raise up seed unto his brother. There were therefore seven brethren: and the first took a wife, and died without children. And the second took her to wife, and he died childless. And the third took her; and in

like manner the seven also: and they left no children, and died. Last of all the woman died also. Therefore in the resurrection whose wife of them is she? For seven had her to wife. And Jesus answering said unto them, The children of this world marry, and are given in marriage: But they which shall be accounted worthy to obtain that world, and the resurrection from the dead, neither marry, nor are given in marriage: Neither can they die any more: for they are equal unto the angels; and are the children of God, being the children of the resurrection. Now that the dead are raised, even Moses shewed at the bush, when he calleth the Lord the God of Abraham, and the God of Isaac, and the God of Jacob. For he is not a God of the dead, but of the living: for all live unto him. Then certain of the scribes answering said, Master, thou hast well said. And after that they durst not ask him any question at all"

Jesus answers the Sadducee's improbable question by referring to scripture from the first five books of the Old Testament called the *Pentateuch*, stating that *"even Moses showed us at the burning bush."* In reference to the fact that Moses spoke of God calling Him the God of Abraham, the God of Isaac, and the God of Jacob. He is not a God of the dead, but the living: for all live unto Him.

The *Pentateuch* is the Greek name given to the first five books of the Old Testament. The word *Pente* means five, and Teuchos means book or volume. Therefore, it represents a five-volume book. The books are Genesis, Exodus, Leviticus, Numbers, and Deuteronomy. They are also referred to as the five books of Moses. The Jews call these books the *'Torah,'* or the law, originally consisting of one scroll.

Other names for these books in the Old Testament are;

- The law
- The book of the law
- The book of the law of Moses
- The book of Moses
- The law of the Lord
- The law of God
- The book of the law of God
- The book of the law of the Lord
- The book of the law of the Lord their God
- The law of Moses the Servant of God

The Hebrews named each section of the Pentateuch following a Mesopotamian custom of using the first few words of each book to describe it.

This resulted in the following;
Genesis = In the beginning *'Bereshith'*

Exodus = And these are the names of *'We'elleh shemoth'*

Leviticus = And He called *'Wayyiqra'*

Numbers = In the wilderness (This was actually the fifth word) *'bemidbar'*

Deuteronomy = These are the words *'Elle debharim'*

Of course, these were not meant to be official titles for the books but a method of describing the scroll section.

The Sadducees would not have listened to any other quote because they believed that only the first five books of the Old Testament (The Pentateuch) were divinely inspired scripture. Jesus was sure to quote from those scriptures alone.

Making His point scripturally to the Sadducees, we see in verse 40 they had nothing left to say.

So we know by what Jesus says here to the Sadducees that there is a spirit that leaves the body when we die, and we continue to exist outside our bodies.

I worked with a friend of mine around 2000, who, in a simple conversation one day, stated to me, *"Once you die, you just don't exist anymore."*

This is a remarkable statement for those who know they are corrupt and feel this need to sear their conscience because they can not stand the guilt and condemnation they feel inside or the thought of having to answer for the things they have done in their lives.

This frees a person to live how *THEY* wish and do the things *THEY* want without ever having to be held responsible by any higher power for their behavior or actions.

This is the height of selfishness; this mentality plagues our country today. Everything is always someone else's fault. "Don't blame me!", "It's not my fault!"

We see examples of this all the time. "It's not my fault I'm getting in trouble in school; I have ADD, ADHD, ABC & 123!"

Blame a handful of random letters and call the doctor for medication so Little Johnny won't set the school bathroom on fire anymore.

Now I'm not implying that there is no such thing as a chemical imbalance or severe medical conditions which do require medications. But I am saying that I see more children each year get medicated in our school systems as a means of control instead of raising them in a proper environment with adequate discipline and love.

But it is not just the children who choose to use scapegoats. They have learned it from us adults who have an excuse for everything. If you have ever watched the news, then you have had an opportunity to see court trials and outstanding Defense Lawyers. They have made careers out of attributing their client's behavior, condition, and circumstance to everything except their client!

I am sure it has happened somewhere, but just once in my life, I would LOVE to see someone go to the stand and say, "Yes, your honor, I did it. It was my fault, and I was wrong! I will accept whatever punishment our law requires for the crimes I have committed."

On the last day, we will have no lawyer, just a judge. We will have no excuse, just a sentence. Unless you accept Christ, you WILL be found guilty, regardless; in fact, you are already guilty unless you have Jesus.

Not because you were raised in a Godless home. Not because you were abused as a child. Not because you grew up on welfare and felt you had to live a criminal life to survive. But you will be guilty of not accepting our Lord Jesus Christ. And you will not be allowed into Heaven to spend eternity with Him.

Many scripture references in the Bible explain that there *IS* life after death. That is the whole point of the Bible so that we can allow Christ into our lives and secure our eternity.

2 Timothy 4:6
"For I am now ready to be offered, and the time of my departure is at hand."

We read in Timothy the Apostle Paul explaining that he is about to leave this place, going on to the next.

Acts 5:10
"Then fell she down straightway at his feet, and yielded up the ghost: and the young men came in, and found her dead, and, carrying her forth, buried her by her husband."

Here we read that when Ananias' wife, Sapphira, fell dead, she gave up the ghost. Her spirit left her body.

But where does the spirit go when it leaves the body? Even non-Christians know of fundamental theology: the good go to heaven, and the wicked go to hell. But we will get into that in later chapters. First, I want to talk about why we have to die.

Death is the punishment for sin. This death sentence was handed down from Adam and Eve because they sinned against God.

They were told this would happen if they ate from the tree, and we must surely die because they ate from the tree.

When this is over, there will be a new heaven, earth, and Jerusalem, and we will have new bodies.

Why? Because sin has touched heaven, earth, Jerusalem, and our flesh.

When this is all over, and we are with the Lord for the rest of eternity, God wants us to be in a place that has never been touched by sin.

So after judgment, when sin, death, the false prophet, anti-Christ, and beast are cast into Gehenna, along with the fallen angels and all those who do not accept Jesus Christ as their atoning sacrifice to pay the debt incurred by the Law, there will be no more sin.

God will create a new heaven, new earth, new Jerusalem, and new bodies so there will be perfection all around us.

There are many references to death in the Bible. Of course, we are talking about physical death right now. Still, there is also spiritual death and eternal death, the penal consequence for sin, also called the second death.

You can open the Bible in just about any chapter and find some teaching on the spirit, death, and the afterlife, either in Heaven with the Lord or in damnation.

To answer where the departed spirits went, specifically when they died in the Old Testament, we need to read on to the next chapter and discover what the Bible has to say about the abodes of the departed spirits.

[CHAPTER FOUR]

SHEOL – Abode of the Departed Spirits

One of the most significant problems with understanding heaven & hell is that most people read the King James Version of the Holy Bible.

Although this is a trusted translation, the translators chose to simplify the text by using the same English word for many different Hebrew and Greek words.

This is done through the Bible with words like love, heaven, hell, etc., replacing multiple different Hebrew and Greek words with various meanings, with English words that are less descriptive and do not always define the term it is replacing.

Some of the newer prints of the King James Version and some NIV and Amplified Bibles will note the translation differences.

I have an NIV Bible that annotates the word *hell,* for instance, and in the margin, it says 'the pit.' This makes understanding scripture so much easier.

You could opt for a literal translation bible, such as Young's Literal. They are more expensive but well worth the cost.

Another option would be to purchase an expositor's bible. These can be expensive but well worth the expense.

Another option would be to learn Hebrew and Greek, which is tedious, complicated, and redundant if you use the available study tools and guides.

Suppose your Bible does not have the annotations feature or something similar. In that case, I suggest getting either a study Bible or perhaps a concordance to ensure a proper understanding of scripture during your studies.

The majority of the scriptures in the Holy Bible, they keep their general meaning in the King James Version. Therefore, when you want to search the scriptures for a more in-depth understanding, you need to arm yourself with study tools.

Here are some examples of the actual differences found in the King James Bible when examined with the original Hebrew and Greek texts, remembering that when reference is made to *Original Hebrew and Greek texts,* it is about the oldest known copies which have been compared for accuracy.

EXAMPLE:
Many different Greek words describe various types of love.

Âhab - Means to have affection for.

Dôwd - Means a beloved friend, uncle, or relative.

Agâbâh - Means to love amorously.

Agapao - Means to love in a social or moral sense.

Thelo - Means to desire.

Philadelphia - Means brotherly love.

Philoteknos - Means the love of children.

All of these different words for love with different meanings were translated into the single English word 'love.' This can cause confusion when searching the word but can outright be inappropriate if the words are misapplied. One can only wonder how often we have misunderstood the true meaning of love in our culture, then turned to scripture to try and understand God's love without an understanding of translation.

We see the same thing happen with the English word *'hell.'* It is generically used for Hebrew and Greek words in the Holy Bible, such as Sheol, Hades, Gehenna, Torment, Paradise, Abraham's, Bosom, and Tartarus.

All names of different places have different meanings and functions, yet all are translated into the one English word, hell.

So to better understand what hell is, we need to understand what each of the original terms represents.

Sheol (Lit) - Abode of the dead (or departed spirits).

- Mentioned 65 times in the Old Testament

- 31 times King James translates *Sheol* into *hell*

- 31 times King James translates *Sheol* into *grave*

- 3 times King James translates *Sheol* into *the pit*

In ordinary usage, it means ravine, chasm, underworld, or world of the dead.

In the Old Testament, it is the place where the dead have their abode, a hollow space underneath the earth where the dead are gathered in.

In the New Testament, Sheol is referred to as "Hades" because that is the closest Greek translation of the word. And it is mentioned 42 times in the New Testament.

We see that 31 times King James translators translated *Sheol* into the word *grave.* But the Hebrew word for *grave* is altogether different than the Hebrew word *Sheol.* But the translators chose the word *grave* anyway.

The Hebrew word for grave is *qeber,* not *Sheol*. *Qeber* is defined as a sepulcher: a burying place or grave. This is where the *physical bodies* of the dead go. *Qeber* is used many times in the plural, showing that there can be *many* of them. i.e., many graves.

We often read in the scriptures of a person *having* a '*qeber*.' So we know from the original Hebrew that a grave (*qeber*) is where the *physical bodies* of the dead go.

We also read of *ownership* of a *qeber*. These points show evidence that the English word *grave* is an incorrect translation of the Hebrew word *Sheol,* thus causing confusion about where our *souls* go when we die.

I have heard many times, from many people, the theological point of view that when we die, we 'wait in the grave' until Christ comes. Well, reading the King James Version without an understanding of the original Hebrew and Greek and not understanding the translator's dilemma with the limitations of the English language, I can see where you would arrive at this conclusion, although incorrect as it is.

But common sense and reading of the scriptures show this theological idea to be contrary to scripture and Christ's teachings.

For instance, if we are to 'wait in the grave' for the appearance of Christ, why did

Jesus tell the thief on the cross in ***Luke 23:43,*** *"And Jesus said unto him, Verily I say unto thee, Today shalt thou be with me in paradise."*

Does this mean that Jesus, too, is waiting in the grave? Or perhaps He was not truthful to make the thief feel at ease in his time of dying?

It makes no sense to believe that we wait in the grave for Christ. Jesus doesn't say, *when I come back for you, then you will be with me in paradise.* Or, *After your in the grave a while, I'll come and wake you up and take you to heaven.*

It's simple; the scriptures teach us in ***2 Corinthians 5:8*** *"We are confident, I say, and willing rather to be absent from the body, and to be present with the Lord."*

The Word of God says nothing about waiting in some magical sleeping beauty state for Christ, our prince, to come and awaken us with a proverbial magic kiss.

The scripture that this false doctrine is derived from is more than likely one of the many references in the Old Testament where people like David are exclaiming that they know their Redeemer lives and will not leave them in the grave.

One problem with this, though. The word is *not* grave in the original Hebrew. It's *Sheol,* which is the abode of the dead, or Abraham's bosom for those who were righteous.

We know from scripture that your spirit is alive, awake, and conscious while you are in Abraham's bosom. The story of the rich man and Lazarus tells us so! But we will talk about that in later chapters.

Righteous Old Testament men *were* waiting for Christ to come because He had not been born yet! They knew that if they were to die *before* He came, that He would not leave them in Abraham's bosom in Sheol but come and take them to be with the Father in heaven.

Until Christ died for us and all of humankind, no one could go to heaven and be with the Father.

John 14:2-6

"In my Father's house are many mansions: if it were not so, I would have told you. I go to prepare a place for you. And if I go and prepare a place for you, I will come again, and receive you unto myself; that where I am, there ye may be also. And whither I go ye know, and the way ye know. Thomas saith unto him, Lord, we know not whither thou goest; and how can we know the way? Jesus saith unto him, I am the way, the truth, and the life: no man cometh unto the Father, but by me."

So scripture tells us that no one can go to heaven where the Father is unless we accept Christ. But no one could accept Christ until He was born and died for us. So everyone before Christ had to wait in Sheol in Abraham's bosom for Christ to die for humankind's sins so they could enter heaven to be with the father.

It's easy to see that belief in a doctrine that teaches we sleep or are unconscious until Christ awakens us is not only contrary to scripture but calls Jesus himself a liar.

Sheol is where the departed spirits in the Old Testament would reside. This is their abode. In the scriptures, the word *Sheol* is *never* used in plural simply because there is only *one Sheol.* We also never read of a person *having* or *owning* a *Sheol.* Therefore, we may conclude from our word study that *qeber (grave)* is a poor translation of the word *Sheol.* You will never read a scripture stating that the *body* is in *Sheol* or the *spirit* is in *qeber.* This proves that *Sheol* *cannot* be a *grave.*

Now we will examine some scriptures to help us understand the usage of Sheol and the function of the place itself.

Job 26:5-6 (Lit)

"The departed spirits and their inhabitants are made to writhe from beneath the waters. Sheol {is} naked before Him, and is no covering for the Place of Ruin."

Here we see Job telling us that Sheol is beneath the waters, perhaps oceans, and even there in the depths, the place of ruin (or torment) has no covering from God.

Here is another example of scripture showing us that we are conscious after death. We see that the departed spirits writhe in *'the place of ruin,'* or Torment. This tells us that Job refers to the torment side, not the opposing side, Abraham's bosom. God sees all, even in the depths of ruin.

Psalms 9:17
"The wicked shall be turned into Sheol, and all the nations that forget God."

We read in psalms a scripture speaking of a place reserved in Sheol for the wicked and all of those who forget God.

This scripture shows that the unrighteous and unfaithful have a destination after death, and it's in the Torment side of Sheol.

Psalms 16:10
"For thou wilt not leave my soul in hell; neither wilt thou suffer thine Holy One to see corruption."

You may be asking yourself, "Why is David's soul going to *hell*?" The answer is he's *not!* The original Hebrew word that is used here is

Sheol, again translated improperly by the translators as *hell.*

David confidently states that God would not leave him in *Sheol.* But being righteous and faithful, David would reside in Abraham's bosom in *Sheol.* This is where he would wait for Christ, and rightly so. As we discussed earlier, no one can go to heaven and be with the father until Jesus died for our sins.

It goes on to say that God will not suffer His Holy One (the righteous and faithful one) to see corruption. So the place reserved for the wicked in Sheol (Torment) is within view of the area reserved for the faithful and righteous (Abraham's bosom) that wait for Christ.

But Christ will not be there long because God will not suffer him to see corruption. So David is showing his faithfulness in Christ and trusting that the savior will one day come and get him from this place in Sheol reserved for the faithful and righteous and take him where he will live in Christ's presence forever (***Psalms 16:11***).

Psalms 86:13

"For great is thy mercy toward me: and thou hast delivered my soul from the lowest hell."

Again, Sheol has been replaced here with the word *hell*. This scripture speaks of Christ's coming and delivering those from Abraham's bosom in Sheol to heaven, not leaving them there for eternity. This was a common theme for the righteous and faithful in the Old Testament. Many times David spoke of his Lord not leaving him in Sheol.

Psalms 88:10-12 (Lit)
"Will you do wonders for the dead? Or will the departed spirits rise {and} thank you? Selah. Will your mercy be declared in the grave? Your faithfulness in {the place of} ruin? Will your wonders be known in the dark, and your righteousness in the land of forgetfulness?"

God is Omnipresent. We are told this many times throughout scripture; He is everywhere.

Deuteronomy 4:39 - *In heaven and on earth*
Isaiah 66:1 – *In heaven and earth*
1 Kings 8:27 – *not limited to just the heavens*
Psalms 139:5-12 – *from up in heaven down to Sheol*
Jeremiah 23:23, 24 – *you cannot hide from God*
Acts 17:27 – *He is close to us all*

Unlike after the judgment, when God's presence is absent from the final lake of fire

(Gehenna) for eternity, God's presence is everywhere, even in Sheol. It is naked before Him.

But all those in torment have already sealed their fate in life; therefore, God's miracles serve no purpose there. Its inhabitants call to the Lord with no avail.

Psalms 139:8 (Lit)
"Where will I go from Your Spirit? Or where from your face will I run away? If I go up to Heaven, there you {are}. If I make my bed in Sheol, look you {are there}!"

We see His presence everywhere. Sheol was translated as Hades in Greek, which later was translated into our modern speech as hell.

Unlike the common understanding of hell, the spirits of all men who died in the Old Testament went to Sheol because it was the gathering place of the dead. Good and evil, where you received rest or torment. It is the journey without return. There are no works that can be done there either. Once you have gone, there is nothing you can do to change that.

Ecclesiastes 9:10 (Lit)
"All that your hand finds to do, with {all} your strength do {it}. For where you go, there is no work, or planning, or knowledge, or wisdom, in Sheol."

We see that no work, planning, knowledge or wisdom will change once you've gone to Sheol (torment or paradise).

Once you have gone to Sheol, you are where you are regardless of anything you say or do.

This scripture alone shows us that no road leads to heaven that runs through hell.

There is no purgatory. You don't go to some holding place until you've worked your way out or get prayed out by living loved ones. This notion is ridiculous because your eternal fate is determined by *your* choices and decisions in life, not by others' prayers after death. Once you die, your destiny has already been sealed.

This is why when the rich man called out from torment to Abraham and Lazarus in paradise for relief, none was given.

This is also why God answers not those in torment. They had their whole life to call on the Lord's name and seek Him and chose not to. Our God is just, and anyone who ends up in torment or Gehenna, in the end, has earned it. God would not unjustly punish those for eternity if they did not deserve it.

In the end, every knee will bow, and every tongue will confess. But it will not change your destination once you have died.

[CHAPTER FIVE]

TORMENT - Abode of the Unrighteous

Torment is the place in Sheol reserved for the departed spirits of the unfaithful and unrighteous.

It is also referred to in scriptures as;

Place of torment.
Place of ruin.
The pit.
The land of forgetfulness (Maybe a reference to ***Psalms 9:17*** – *"The wicked will be turned to Sheol, and all the nations who forget God."*

Numbers 16:30-33
"But if the Lord make a new thing, and the earth open her mouth, and swallow them up, with all that

appertain unto them, and they go down quick into the pit; then ye shall understand that these men have provoked the Lord. And it came to pass, as he had made an end of speaking all these words, that the ground clave asunder that was under them:
And the earth opened her mouth, and swallowed them up, and their houses, and all the men that appertained unto Korah, and all their goods. They, and all that appertained to them, went down alive into the pit, and the earth closed upon them: and they perished from among the congregation."

The families of Dathan and Abiram were swallowed up by the earth, but Korah and his followers were executed. Another sign is that Sheol's pit or torment side is located under the earth.

While Job was going through his trials, he thought he would end up in torment, as we see in the scriptures.

Job 10:21, 22
"Before I go whence I shall not return, even to the land of darkness and the shadow of death; A land of darkness, as darkness itself; and of the shadow of death, without any order, and where the light is as darkness."

He later realized that though he was going through trials, no matter what happened, he would be resurrected one day. Then, the Lord would give him his resurrected body, and he would see God.

Job 19:25, 26
"For I know that my redeemer liveth, and that he shall stand at the latter day upon the earth: And though after my skin worms destroy this body, yet in my flesh shall I see God:"

We know from scripture that God is present even in Sheol, but those in torment cannot speak to Him or of Him to any avail. This is because their life's fate has already been determined and sealed by their death.

Psalms 9:17
"The wicked shall be turned into Sheol, all the nations that forget God."

I believe this is why torment is referred to as the land of forgetfulness because all nations and people who forget God end up in Torment.

Psalms 88:10-12
"Wilt thou shew wonders to the dead? Shall the dead arise and praise thee? Selah. Shall thy lovingkindness be declared in the grave? or thy faithfulness in destruction? Shall thy wonders be

known in the dark? and thy righteousness in the land of forgetfulness?"

What use are miracles to the dead? God uses signs, wonders, and miracles to bring us to Him. But once you have died, your fate is sealed. We know from scripture that there is no salvation in torment. There is no crossing over to paradise. So there is no purpose for God's works, wonders, and miracles in Torment because no one can come to God.

We see this with the rich man and Lazarus when he asks for a bit of water because of his great thirst.

When Jesus told this story, I thought of the Holy Spirit of God and how often He is referred to as water.

I think of Jesus at the well and how He told the woman of water that would not only quench her thirst but she would never thirst again.

The Holy Spirit is not at work in Sheol as He is on earth. Therefore, God's hand is not holding back the forces of evil as He does here.

When Jesus faced Pilate, Pilate said, "Do you not understand that I can have you executed?" Jesus replied, "You can do nothing to me my Father in heaven does not allow."

Job as well, when Satan was going to attack him, God only allowed Satan so much but stopped him short of taking Job's life.

On earth, we have God's hand in control. He holds back even the devil and his attacks on humankind and only allows so much.

Nothing is done that God does not allow on this earth.

But in Sheol, the Spirit of God, His Holy Spirit, is no longer holding back the demonic forces.

And those who find themselves in torment will see themselves receiving the total onslaught of suffering, with no Holy Spirit to restrain them.

This story that Jesus tells about the rich man and Lazarus has a spiritual lesson about the afterlife.

In Sheol, there will be no point in crying out to God because that time has passed. There will be no salvation there, no praise there, no miracles there. Only pain, sadness, darkness, and torment are there.

The only hope for anyone is to call on the name of Jesus NOW, while He can still answer you, to commit yourself to Jesus NOW while He can still come to you and fill you with His Holy Spirit.

Call on the name of the Lord, confess your sins to Him. The Bible promises the Lord is quick to forgive!

Repent of those sins and commit yourself to the Lord, and you will be saved. The Bible promises that!

If you have never done so, you can do it now! You can pray to your Father in heaven, and He will answer your heart.

Praise God!

[CHAPTER SIX]

The Great Gulf – Separating Torment from Paradise

We know from the scriptures that there are two sides to Sheol, Torment (where the unfaithful rich man went) and Paradise (*Abraham's bosom*). And we know they are separated by a great gulf, as described in the story of the rich man and Lazarus.

Luke 16:19-31
"There was a certain rich man, which was clothed in purple and fine linen, and fared sumptuously every day: And there was a certain beggar named Lazarus, which was laid at his gate, full of sores, And desiring to be fed with the crumbs which fell from the rich man's table: moreover the dogs came and licked his sores. And it came to pass, that the beggar died, and was carried by the angels into Abraham's bosom: the rich man also died, and was buried; And in Sheol he

lift up his eyes, being in torments, and seeth Abraham afar off, and Lazarus in his bosom. And he cried and said, Father Abraham, have mercy on me, and send Lazarus, that he may dip the tip of his finger in water, and cool my tongue; for I am tormented in this flame. But Abraham said, Son, remember that thou in thy lifetime receivedst thy good things, and likewise Lazarus evil things: but now he is comforted, and thou art tormented. And beside all this, between us and you there is a great gulf fixed: so that they which would pass from hence to you cannot; neither can they pass to us, that would come from thence. Then he said, I pray thee therefore, father, that thou wouldest send him to my father's house: For I have five brethren; that he may testify unto them, lest they also come into this place of torment. Abraham saith unto him, They have Moses and the prophets; let them hear them. And he said, Nay, father Abraham: but if one went unto them from the dead, they will repent. And he said unto him, If they hear not Moses and the prophets, neither will they be persuaded, though one rose from the dead."

Nothing else is said in the Bible about the great gulf. But from this event recalled by Jesus, we can see that the gulf is impassable, and it separates torment from Abraham's bosom.

[CHAPTER SEVEN]

PARADISE – Abraham's Bosom

Paradise was also called Abraham's bosom and place of rest. When a righteous and faithful man in the Old Testament died, he was said to be gathered unto his people. We see this many times in the Old Testament. But what do we know of Paradise and its true purpose? And do we go straight there, or do we sleep until our resurrection day? Well, the scriptures tell us exactly what happens.

Luke 23:42, 43
"And he said unto Jesus, Lord, remember me when thou comest into thy kingdom. And Jesus said unto him, Verily I say unto thee, Today shalt thou be with me in paradise."

Here we see Christ speaking with the thief on the cross about paradise. This is the thief who confessed he deserved the cross for his sins and believed that Christ was a king. And Jesus responded to him and said that he would be with Him in paradise that day! Jesus said nothing about after you sleep a while or later when you get a resurrected body. Instead, he said, "Today, you will be with me in paradise!"

Luke 16:22, 23
"And it came to pass, that the beggar died, and was carried by the angels into Abraham's bosom: the rich man also died, and was buried. And in Sheol he lift up his eyes, being in torments, and seeth Abraham afar off, and Lazarus in his bosom."

We see in Luke that when a righteous and faithful man dies, he is carried by angels to Abraham's bosom. When the unfaithful and unrighteous man died, he was just buried and opened his eyes in torment. There was no homecoming for the rich man. And there was no slumber for either of them.

The phrase "..And was gathered unto his people" Is used to express the fact that the spirit of the righteous and faithful leaves the body to be with the righteous and faithful spirits of those who died before him.

Genesis 25:8
"Then Abraham gave up the Ghost, and died in a good old age, an old man, and full of years; and was gathered to his people."

Here we see that Abraham's spirit left him, and he (spirit) was gathered to his people.

Genesis 25:17
"And these are the years of the life of Ishmael, an hundred and thirty and seven years: and he gave up the Ghost and died; and was gathered unto his people."

Genesis 35:29
"And Isaac gave up the Ghost, and died, and was gathered unto his people, being old and full of days: and his sons Esau and Jacob buried him."

As you can see in ***Genesis 35:29,*** Isaac was gathered unto his people *BEFORE* his sons Esau and Jacob buried him. This shows us that Isaac's spirit was in Abraham's bosom, gathered unto his people before his body was in the ground.

But what was the purpose of Abraham's bosom in Old Testament times? Why didn't the spirits of the dead just go to heaven? Well, that is simple. God does not change. God will *never* act in contradiction to His word. God's word says the following;

John 14:6
"Jesus saith unto him, I am the way, the truth, and the life: no man cometh unto the Father, but by me."

No man cometh unto the Father, but by Jesus alone. He doesn't say after I die on the cross; from that moment on, you have to accept me to get into heaven.

Jesus tells us here in John that He is the ONLY way to heaven, where the Father is. We have all sinned and are not worthy of heaven. But Christ died for our sins to re-establish the relationship between God and us that was destroyed in the Garden, thus allowing us to enter heaven through Christ.

But until Christ came and died for our sins, becoming the perfect sacrifice and allowing us, through Him, to enter into heaven, the righteous and faithful man needed a waiting place.

God must keep His word, so all who died *BEFORE* the savior who was righteous and faithful had to wait until Christ's sacrifice so they could enter heaven and be with God.

The Old Testament man knew this and understood in faith that they would be waiting for a savior who was to come for them, even though they may not have realized the magnitude of it all, even if he was to come after they died. We see this many times in the Old Testament when writers like David would exclaim, "I know you will not leave me in Sheol!"

Psalms 16:10
"For thou wilt not leave my soul to Sheol; neither wilt thou suffer thy holy one to see corruption."

Here we read a Psalm of David where he expresses that he knows that the Savior will come for him, even after his death. He also states that they won't stay there when the Lord does come for him! We know this because of the statement in scripture saying that God will not suffer thy holy one to see corruption. We know that in Abraham's Bosom in Sheol, it is possible to see Torment across the Great Gulf. So when Christ descends to Paradise, He will take those faithful and righteous ones waiting there for Him to the heavenly paradise where the Father is.

Psalms 49:15
"But God will redeem my soul from the power of Sheol; for he will receive me."

Here we read a Psalm from one of the sons of Korah. They were Levites and doorkeepers to the Temple. They also state that the Savior will come and take them from Sheol.

So Old Testament men knew that if they were to die before the Savior came, they would still be received by Him and taken to be with the Father!

[CHAPTER EIGHT]

PURGATORY - Christ's Sacrifice not Good Enough?

This formal doctrine of 'purgatory' was adopted by the Roman Catholic Church in the 11th century and was shaped at the Council of Trent between 1545 and 1563.

It states that souls who have accepted Jesus Christ but are not evil enough to go to hell go to purgatory, where the debt for unrepented sins is to be purged.

There is absolutely no Biblical basis for this belief. On the contrary, the Bible says the opposite, which means this doctrine contradicts God's word.

The Bible tells us there is no condemnation for those in Jesus Christ.

Romans 8:1

"There is therefore now no condemnation to them which are in Christ Jesus, who walk not after the flesh, but after the Spirit."

This belief in purgatory contradicts the New Testament's teachings of complete redemption of believers by God's grace alone.

Ephesians 2:8
"For by grace are ye saved through faith; and that not of yourselves: it is the gift of God:"

A gift of God! Not something that is earned or deserved but a gift given to us because of God's love and grace.

2 Timothy 1:9
"Who hath saved us, and called us with an holy calling, not according to our works, but according to his own purpose and grace, which was given us in Christ Jesus before the world began,"

The Roman Catholic Church claims the 6th-century concept under Pope Gregory I in 2 Maccabees 12:43-46 as "proof text" for purgatory.

However, this is *NOT* part of the Holy Scriptures, but part of a collection of scriptures called the "Apocrypha," which was never recognized or considered scripture by the early Jews, Christians, the Church, or even Jesus Himself.

This doctrine is absurd. The road to Heaven does not run through hell (a purgatory of suffering).

This doctrine is unscriptural, but there is no possible need for purgatory, a place of purification. The Bible says, "the blood of Jesus Christ, His Son, cleanseth us from all sin." ***1 John 1:7***

[CHAPTER NINE]

THE ABYSS - Dark Underworld

Strong's Reference #12;
It means depthless, infernal, and bottomless. It is presided over by "Abaddon, the prince of the pit." It is described as immeasurable deep or underworld.

Revelation 9:11
"They have over them as king the angel of the abyss: his name in Hebrew is Abaddon, and in the Greek tongue he hath the name Apollyon."

Abaddon literally means "place of destruction." But it is used as a name here in revelation. Moreover, the same word appears only once in the New Testament in its Greek equivalent, Apollyon.

Here the idea of destruction is personified as the "angel from the bottomless pit," so the word is often translated as "destroyer." Abaddon (or Apollyon) is the angel reigning over the realm of the dead, who appeared after the fifth trumpet in John's vision.

There really is not a lot of information on the Abyss. Other mentions of the pit can be found in the following scriptures;

In the Literal Translation, these scriptures refer to the abyss as the pit.

Revelation 11:7
Revelation 17:8
Revelation 20:1
Revelation 20:3

[CHAPTER TEN]

TARTARUS – Abode of Fallen Angels

Strong's Reference #5020;

Tartarus means the deepest abyss of Sheol and to incarcerate in eternal torment. Greek texts refer to it as the pit of the pit (*Revelation 9:1*) and the pit of the abyss (*Revelation 9:2*).

2 *Peter* 2:4

"For if God did not spare angels when they sinned, but cast them down to Tartarus, and committed them to chains of darkness, and reserved them for judgment;"

Here we see Tartarus referred to as chains of darkness where they (fallen Angels) are to be held until judgment. We see that the fifth trumpet of judgment has been sounded in *Revelation 9:1* before an Angel with a key opens the pit of the pit.

Jude 1:6
"And angels who had not kept their own original state, but had abandoned their own dwelling, he keeps in eternal chains under gloomy darkness, to the judgment of the great day;."

Here we see another reference to the angels cast down to Tartarus (eternal chains under gloomy darkness - or Abyss) until the judgment of the great day of Tribulation.

Revelation 9:1
"And the fifth angel sounded, and I saw a star from heaven fallen unto the earth: and there was given to him the key of the pit of the abyss."

We see here that after the 5th trumpet sounded, an angel with the key to the pit of the abyss (which is Tartarus) came down to earth to open the pit. Reading on, we see that locusts (which are symbolic of destruction but refer to fallen angels being released from Tartarus in this case) were released on the earth and poured out, but they had limitations. They were only allowed to torment a person for five months, showing that they were still under God's authority though they were released.

This is the judgment scriptures refer to when they speak of the angels being held in chains.

Though Tartarus is mentioned once by name and once by reference, a lot is not needed to be known except what we are told. Angels are there for sinning against God and won't be released until judgment on earth at Tribulation.

[CHAPTER ELEVEN]

WHAT IS HEAVEN TO OLD TESTAMENT MAN?

Of course, we will see the same problems with the King James Version of heaven as we saw with hell.

Just as the King James Version gives one generic translation word 'hell' to so many different Hebrew and Greek words, they did the same for heaven.

Hashamayim (HEB) - This is the place above where the celestial bodies revolve.

Hayamiym (HEB) - The sky where there are clouds.

Ouranos (GRK) - The same as Hashamayim but acknowledging the presence of Jesus there (Abode of God).

Ouranothen (GRK) - From the sky or from heaven.

Epouranios (GRK) - Above the sky or celestial.

Nehemiah 9:6
"Thou, even thou, art Lord alone; thou hast made heaven, the heaven of heavens, with all their host, the earth, and all things that are therein, the seas, and all that is therein, and thou preservest them all; and the host of heaven worshippeth thee."

Here we see a scripture using both forms of the Hebrew word Shamayim, first, as a reference to the place above where celestial bodies revolve (Hashamayim), then as the place above where the sky and clouds are (Hayamiym). To add to the confusion, King James translators used the same word, 'heaven,' to translate the five different words relating to other heavens.

Luke 15:7
"I say unto you, that likewise joy shall be in heaven over one sinner that repenteth, more than over ninety and nine just persons, which need no repentance."

Here the original Greek word for heaven was Ouranos, which we see is used when speaking of the third heaven in the New

Testament, acknowledging that Christ is now there. Likewise, the Hebrew words used in reference to the third heaven before the Crucifixion recognize the place. Still, they do not speak of the residency of God.

Hebrews 8:1
"Now of the things which we have spoken this is the sum: We have such an high priest, who is set on the right hand of the throne of the Majesty in the heavens;"

Again the Greek word Ouranos is used, acknowledging the presence of God in the third heaven.

2 Corinthians 12:1-5
"It is not expedient for me doubtless to glory (LIT. - to boast indeed is not profitable to me.). I will come to visions and revelations of the Lord. I knew a man in Christ above fourteen years ago, (whether in the body, I cannot tell; or whether out of the body, I cannot tell: God knoweth ;) such an one caught up to the third heaven (Strong's Ref. # 3772 – as the abode of God). And I knew such a man, (whether in the body, or out of the body, I cannot tell: God knoweth;) How that he was caught up into paradise (Strong's Ref. # 3857 – place of future happiness, Eden), and heard unspeakable words, which it is not lawful for a man

to utter. Of such an one will I glory: yet of myself I will not glory, but in mine infirmities."

A few interesting points about this scripture: first, we see Paul speaking of himself in the third person. We see in verse 5 that he is talking of himself in the third person to not boast of what he has seen and heard in paradise, to keep himself from becoming prideful. Secondly, the word for heaven here is the Greek word Ouranos which means the Lord was there in heaven. And we see that Paradise is now in the third heaven, as opposed to being in Sheol, where it was before Christ was crucified.

3rd Heaven - Beyond Space (Created FIRST) Abode of God

Genesis 1:1
"In the beginning God created the heaven (His abode) and the earth (our abode)."

The word King James translated for heaven here is Hashamayim (Strong's #8064), meaning higher than the celestial bodies revolve.

1st Heaven - Sky (Created SECOND)

Genesis 1:6-8

"And God said, Let there be a firmament (expanse) *in the midst of the waters, and let it divide the waters from the waters. And God made the firmament, and divided the waters which were under the firmament* (oceans, seas, lakes, etc...) *from the waters which were above the firmament* (the waters that once surrounded the earth before the flood which created the greenhouse-like environment for the earth)*: and it was so. And God called the firmament* (expanse) *Heaven* (sky)*. And the evening and the morning were the second day."*

We see here that before the flood, a layer of water surrounded our planet. This would explain how it was able to rain for 40 days and nights, flooding the entire earth. It also makes sense that God perhaps used a giant meteor to hit the earth, thus causing the water layer around the planet to fall as rain and knock the earth off its axis, causing our seasons that did not exist before the flood. This also explains why our magnetic north is different from our axis north.

Acts 14:17

"Nevertheless he left not himself without witness, in that he did good, and gave us rain from heaven (LIT -

from the sky*), and fruitful seasons, filling our hearts with food and gladness."*

2nd Heaven - Outer Space (Created THIRD)

Genesis 1:14-17

"And God said, Let there be lights in the firmament (expanse*) of the heaven* (space*) to divide the day from the night; and let them be for signs, and for seasons, and for days, and years: And let them be for lights in the firmament* (expanse*) of the heaven* (space*) to give light upon the earth: and it was so. And God made two great lights; the greater* (our sun*) light to rule the day, and the lesser* (our moon*) light to rule the night: he made the stars also. And God set them in the firmament* (expanse*) of the heaven* (space*) to give light upon the earth,"*

Ephesians 6:12 (HEB)

"Because we don't wrestle against blood and flesh, but against the rulers, authorities, and the world's rulers of the darkness. Against these spiritual powers of evil in the heavenlies."

Here the word for heaven is Epouranios which means above the sky, which would be space. Once we better understand the different heavens mentioned in the scriptures, we can better understand which heaven the scriptures are referring to. This makes it easier to understand the truth that God is telling us about where we are and where we're going.

[CHAPTER TWELVE]

CONCLUSION

The Old Testament man could be assured of one thing; if he were faithful to the Lord, he would be gathered unto his people when he died in Sheol, the place of departed spirits.

There, in Sheol, he would be carried by angels to paradise, which as also called Abraham's bosom.

While he was in Paradise, he had assurance from the Word of God that a Savior was coming. And he knew that this Christ, this Savior, would not leave him in Sheol but take him to be with the Father in Heaven for eternity.

Jesus, who had not yet died on the cross, told the thief next to Him, "Today you will be with me in Paradise."

Jesus told the man this because the man had received his Salvation from the Lord that day on the cross next to Jesus.

The man confessed he was a sinner and deserved to be on the cross. He also admitted that Jesus was innocent and should not have been on the cross. Finally, he acknowledged that Jesus was God and asked if Jesus would remember him when He came into His kingdom.

Because he confessed his sin, acknowledged Jesus was God, and asked Jesus to remember him in His kingdom, Jesus forgave the man and received him into the Kingdom because of Faith.

The gift of Salvation is just that, a gift. You can not earn it, and no one deserves it, yet because of Jesus' sacrifice and His payment of our debt, we can be seen as justified before the eyes of God.

We become innocent because our debt has been paid for with a perfect atoning sacrifice.

Each of us, the thieves on those crosses that day on either side of Jesus. Both were guilty, for we are all born into the first covenant, which is the Law.

We know by the scriptures that no man is justified but guilty by the Law. Therefore, Jesus said, "I did not come to condemn the world, for they are already condemned, but I came to save it."

By confessing that we are guilty according to the Law we are born under and acknowledging that Jesus is God and that He died to pay the debt, we have incurred by the Law, which states that the penalty for sin is death, we too can receive that gift by faith.

Or we can live our lives as the second thief, who met Jesus on the same day as the repentant thief.

We could mock Jesus with the way we live our lives, acting as if we have no conscience and like there will be no judgment.

Just as it was on the day of Christ's crucifixion, we, too, will stand before the Lord, but this will not be a time to repent but a time for us to receive our judgment.

Will your judgment be, "Well done, good and faithful servant," or will it be, "I do not know you."?

If you have never confessed that you are a sinner, you can do so now. We all are. We are born under the first covenant, which is the Law, and no man can keep the Law.

We know that no man is justified by the Law, and Jesus explained that the Law could not be kept by man.

In the Sermon on the Mount, Jesus said, "If you even look with lust in your heart, you have committed adultery. If you hate your brother, it is the same as murder."

We are all guilty and need to confess that to the Lord. And repent of our sins. That is, turn away from them. ***(Romans 3:10)***

Confession without this repentance will leave you in a state of Unforgiveness. You must not only confess but repent to be forgiven. ***(Acts 17:30)***

Acknowledge that Jesus is God, and ask for His forgiveness. ***(Romans 10:9-10)***

By faith, you will receive Salvation and be counted among the Saints! ***(Romans 10:13)***

Commit yourself, your life, your heart, and your mind to Jesus Christ, and He will give you the promise of the Father. The Holy Spirit, who will indwell within you and give you the gifts and fruits of the Spirit, and you will become a Child of God.

And it all begins not with cleaning up your life first but confessing that it is a mess.

It is God's will that all come to a knowledge of the Truth and Salvation, which can only happen through Jesus Christ. If you have never done so before, pray the following prayer;

Dear God, I know I am a sinner and need your forgiveness.

I believe Jesus shed His blood on the cross to pay the debt owed because of my sin.

I am willing to turn from this sin.

I want Jesus Christ to come into my heart and life as my Savior.

It's that simple. If you trust Jesus as your Savior and commit yourself to Him, you have just begun a wonderful new life with Him.

Read your Bible, talk to God in prayer, and get into a local church that believes in the Word of God and is based on the Bible, founded on Christ, and committed to the Word of God and the Great Commission of Christ.

Amen!

Heaven & Hell

Other books by Pastor Bruce A. Shields

Pandemic Dawn Book I
Rise of the State: Pandemic Dawn Book II
Day of Abomination: Pandemic Dawn Book III
Before the Sun Sets: Pandemic Dawn Book IV

Losing Dani Strumm

HOFC Minister's Manual

Over 800 sermons at
www.TruthDigest,org

HOFC
www.PS127.org

Pastor B. A. Shields Author Website
www.BruceShields.us

Made in the USA
Middletown, DE
15 October 2022

12827103R00066